79,

Alena Kre

JEWISH
cookery

**SLOVART
PUBLISHING**

THE SPIRITUAL DIMENSION OF JEWISH COOKING

There is hardly any other culture in which the preparation and consumption of food has so profound a spiritual dimension and is so fully integrated into ritual as it is in Judaism. The main principles of Jewish cuisine derive from a set of very precise ritual rules known as the *kashrut*. The fundamental principle is the division of animals into edible and inedible from the aspect of ritual cleanliness. The Hebrew word *kosher* means clean or pure, beneficial, worthy, permitted, and its opposite is *trejf* from the Hebrew *terefah* meaning "torn", which originally simply meant animals torn apart by predators, but which came to mean everything that is not kosher. The requirements of *kashrut* are met by animals that have cloven hooves and chew the cud (cattle, sheep, goats, deer), and poultry and fish that have fins and scales, such as carp, trout, tench or salmon. Forbidden species include pigs, horses, all amphibians, reptiles, molluscs, eels and sturgeon (including caviar) among fish.

The principles of *kashrut* also guide the preparation of food. In a kosher kitchen the commandment in the Torah for dairy and meat products to be kept separate is observed punctiliously. Milk symbolises youth and purity, while the meat of a slaughtered animal is a symbol of death, and this is why it is forbidden to eat a dish that contains both milk and meat or to consume meat dishes immediately after dairy dishes. Households even keep two separate sets of plates, cutlery and napkins for the consumption of dairy and meat products. The principles of *kashrut* require ritual slaughter: the *schochet* – the butcher licensed to slaughter animals and poultry according to *kashrut* rules, must drain the blood from the meat. The blood of animals is considered to be their soul, and may not be consumed.

Religious festivals offer the Jewish housewife the best opportunities to show her ingenuity and skill, and the traditional dishes also symbolically express many religious and historical aspects of the festivals themselves. On the Sabbath table the two loaves of challah (the bread in braided

rolls that is also known as barches from the Hebrew *berach,*
blessing), for example, symbolise the double portion of
manna that the Lord sent down to the Israelites in the desert
every Friday, so that there should be enough left over for the
Sabbath. On Rosh Hashanah, the Jewish New Year, the
challah is dipped not in salt as on the Sabbath, but in honey
– so that the ensuing year will be good and sweet. On
Chanukah, the Festival of Lights, the food is fried in oil in
memory of the miracle that occurred after Judas Maccabeus
conquered Jerusalem and revived the worship in the
Temple, dedicating it again to the Lord. Although only
a tiny amount of oil was to be found, it proved enough to
keep the temple menorah, or eight-branched candlestick,
alight for a whole eight days. The hamantaschen cakes
that are baked for Purim, a festival commemorating the
liberation of the Jews in the Persian Empire from the
power of the steward Haman, are shaped to resemble
Haman's three-pointed hat. Another Jewish festival is
Pessach (Passover) in the Spring. At this feast Jews annually
relive the exodus from Egypt, and all the dishes made for
the ritual seder dinner are reminders of the events of this
biblical story. Matzos bread is the symbol of the unleavened
bread that the Israelites ate in the desert. A lamb bone
represents the Passover sacrifice, while charoset (a mixture
of grated apple, nuts, almonds, raisins, cinnamon and sweet
wine) symbolises the clay from which the Jews in Egypt
made bricks. The bitter herbs known as maror (the
traditional ingredients are horseradish, watercress or
endive) represent the bitterness of Egyptian captivity, and so
on and so forth.

Jewish dishes come from all over the world wherever
Jews have found refuge during the long centuries of
diaspora. The local differences and traditions of other
nations have therefore contributed to the enormous diversity
of Jewish cooking. Central and Eastern Europe was the
home of the Ashkenazi Jews, and most of the recipes in this
book are from this area. Many of the dishes will prove an
interesting and tasty addition to the menu even for readers
who are encountering the world of the strict rules and
principles of Jewish cooking for the first time.

G IPIKLTE FISCH
(MARINADED FISH)

1 cup water

1 cup vinegar

4 onions

4 bay leaves

12 peppercorns

1/2 teaspoon mustard seeds

8 grains of allspice

about 1 tablespoon salt

1 carp (weighing about 1 1/2 kg)

vegetables for garnish

Put the water, vinegar, sliced onions, spices and salt in a pan and bring to the boil. Add the carp cut into small portions and simmer for about 20 minutes (at only 80–85°C), until the fish is soft. Remove pan from heat and leave to cool. Then carefully lift the fish portions and onions out of the liquid with a ladle and place in glass bowl. Strain the liquid, pour it over the fish and leave to marinade in the fridge for 48 hours. The marinaded fish will keep in the fridge for at least 2 weeks and its flavour improves each day. Serve garnished with fresh or boiled vegetables and parsley or spring onions.

G EHAKTE HERINK
(CHOPPED SALTED HERRING)

3 large salted herrings

1 small onion

1 apple

2 hard-boiled eggs

3 slices of white bread

1 teaspoon sugar

2 tablespoons oil

3 tablespoons vinegar

olives and vegetables for garnish

Let the herrings soak in cold water in a cool place for at least 12 hours to get rid of excess salt. Then clean them, remove skin and bones, and mince or finely chop with the onion, the cored but not peeled apple and the eggs. Remove the crust from the bread, dip in cold water and squeeze out. Then rub the slices well with the sugar, oil and vinegar. Mix the bread into the herring, onion, apple and egg mixture and leave for 3 hours in the fridge. Serve the chopped herring with a garnish of black or green olives and sliced vegetables, such as sweet peppers, tomatoes, lettuce or spring onions.

Fish is an integral part of Jewish cuisine. The rules of the kosher kitchen forbid the serving of fish at the same time as meat, and fish and meat may not be placed side by side on a plate. When meat is served after a fish hors d'oeuvre, the fish should properly be eaten with a piece of bread.

Photo: Gipiklte fisch

G EHAKTE LEBER
(JEWISH CAVIAR)

Fry the livers in half the oil and remove them from the pan. Add the remaining oil and fry the sliced onions until golden. Mince the liver, onion and eggs together and stir in the chicken fat in a bowl. Add salt and pepper to taste and leave to chill in the fridge for at least 2 hours before serving. Jewish caviar is usually served with bread and fresh sliced vegetables or pickles.

1 tablespoon oil

1/2 kg chicken liver

2 onions

2 hard-boiled eggs

3 tablespoons chicken fat

salt and ground pepper

vegetables for garnish

H ERINK SALAT
(SALTED HERRING SALAD)

Remove excess liquid and skin, and bone the herrings. Then chop them into 1.5-cm pieces, and mix with the peeled diced potatoes and apples, sliced cucumber and onion. Add the mayonnaise, sour cream, sugar and vinegar, and pepper to taste, and mix well. Finally lightly stir in the chopped parsley or dill. Serve on lettuce leaves garnished with green olives and cucumber segments.

2 large salted herrings

2 potatoes boiled in their skins

2 apples

1–2 sterilised cucumbers

1 tablespoon finely chopped onion

1/2 cup mayonnaise

1/2 cup sour cream

about 1 teaspoon sugar

4 tablespoons vinegar

ground pepper

1 tablespoon chopped parsley or dill

lettuce, olives and cucumbers for garnish

Pork fat is absolutely forbidden in Jewish cooking. The food is therefore prepared with vegetable oil or chicken, goose or duck fat. Remove the fat from the poultry, cut it into pieces, season with salt and slowly melt in a pan over a low heat. When it is nearly ready add slices of onion and fry until golden. Then remove the onion, pour off the fat and dry the pieces of crackling skin (gribenes).

Photo: Gehakte leber (below) and Herink salat

7

GOLDENE JOJCH (GOLDEN SOUP)

1 chicken (weighing about 2 kg)
4 l water
about 2 teaspoons salt
7 peppecorns
3 grains of allspice
2 onions
1 parsley root
2 carrots
1/4 small celeriac
1–2 tablespoons of oil
2 sprigs parsley
2 springs dill
ground pepper

Put the chicken in a deep pan and add the cold water, salt and pepper. Bring to the boil, reduce temperature and simmer gently for about 40 minutes. Then fry the finely sliced onion and root vegetables until golden and add to the soup. Continue to simmer until the chicken is cooked. Season at the end with finely chopped parsley and dill, pepper and if necessary extra salt to taste. Remove the chicken, cut it into small pieces and replace. Ideally the soup should be garnished with home-made noodles or matzos ball dumplings. It can also be served with kreplach – pirozhki stuffed with chicken.

MATZO KNEIDLACH (MATZO DUMPLINGS)

2 eggs
3 tablespoons poultry fat
1 cup matzo meal
about 1 teaspoon salt
1–2 teaspoons ground ginger
1/2 cup stock

Mix the egg yolks into the warm melted poultry fat and add to the matzo meal mixed with the salt and ginger. Pour on the warm stock and mix well. Beat the egg whites to a stiff consistency and fold in lightly. Leave the mixture to chill in the fridge for about an hour. Then, using wet hands form the mixture into small round walnut-sized balls and boil gently in salted water for about 25 minutes. Matzo dumplings can be served in chicken or beef soup, or as an accompaniment to stewed or roast meat.

Matzo is the unleavened bread that is eaten at Pesach (Passover) when it is forbidden to eat anything leavened. Before Pesach all pastries or bread made of yeast dough must be removed from the house down to the last crumb. Matzo is made from wheat flour in a way that prevents the leavening process – there must be no more than 18 minutes between mixing the flour with the water and baking the bread.

Photo: Goldene jojch with Matzo kneidlach

Borsch with Beef

Place the meat in the boiling salted water, bring back to the boil, reduce the temperature and cook slowly for about 2 hours until tender (remove any dark scum after bringing back to the boil, but leave the white foam, which will disappear during cooking). Remove the meat, cut it into pieces and replace in the pan. Add the peeled and coarsely grated beetroot, the finely chopped onion and crushed garlic, and cook for at least another 20 minutes. Flavour the soup with the lemon juice, sugar, marjoram and salt to taste. Cook for a further approx. 30 minutes. Finally strain the borsch and carefully add the egg yolks (beat them first in a little of the borsch that you have allowed to cool). The borsch can be garnished with chopped parsley or chives.

1 kg prime beef

about 2 teaspoons salt

3 l water

6 medium large beetroot

2 onion

2 cloves of garlic

5 teaspoons lemon juice

2–3 teaspoons sugar

1 teaspoon marjoram

2 egg yolks

parsley or chives for garnish

Krupnik

Put the peeled and chopped tomatoes, finely chopped onion, celeriac with tops, parsley, beans (soaked over night) and dried mushrooms (soaked in water for 15 minutes) into a pan with the water and simmer slowly for about an hour until almost soft. Then add the chopped carrot and dill, season with salt and pepper and simmer for another 20 minutes. If the soup is too thick, add a little more hot water as it cooks to thin it out.

250 g tomatoes

1 onion

2 tablespoons finely chopped celeriac with green tops

1 tablespoons finely chopped parsley

1/4 cup white beans

1/4 cup groats or barley

about 1 cup dried mushrooms

1 l water

1 small carrot

1 tablespoon chopped dill

salt and ground pepper

Vegetables, fruit, eggs, mushrooms, grains, pulses and some kinds of sweets and drinks are known as "parve" or neutral food, which means that they are neither milk nor meat and can therefore be parts of meat or milk dishes.

Photo: Borsch (above) and Krupnik

11

G EFILTE FISCH (STUFFED FISH)

1 carp weighing 2–3 kg

salt

Stuffing:

fish fillet

3 onions

1 tablespoon oil

3 eggs

1 cup breadcrumbs or 3/4 cup matzo meal

1/2 cup water

about 1 teaspoon salt

about 1 teaspoon ground pepper

about 1 teaspoon sugar

Stock:

fish head, fins, tail and bones

2–3 carrots

2–3 teaspoons salt

1/2 teaspoon ground pepper

about 1 teaspoon sugar

Gut the fish, remove head, fins and tail, clean and cut into 3–4 cm pieces. Season with salt and set aside for about 30 minutes. Then carefully remove the flesh without damaging the skin. Make sure to remove all the bones from the flesh. Then mince the flesh, and add the chopped onion lightly browned in oil, the eggs, breadcrumbs or matzo meal, cold water, salt, ground pepper and sugar. Mix well and stuff the sections of fish skin, securing them at the top with toothpicks. Put the fish head, fins, tail and bones in a pan. Barely cover with water, add sliced carrot, salt, pepper and sugar and simmer gently for about 30 minutes. Strain off the stock and set aside the carrot for garnish. Put the stuffed fish portions in a pan, pour over the stock and simmer for about 30 minutes. Carefully lift the portions out with a ladle. Strain the stock again, pour it over the fish, garnish with carrot and place in the fridge to set.

Variation: Try a different stuffing. Mix the minced fish flesh with 1 finely chopped onion, 2 eggs, 1 boiled and blended yolk, 1 medium-sized boiled and grated beetroot, 2 tablespoons grated horseradish and about 1 teaspoon salt.

Gefilte fish is a traditional dish prepared for the Sabbath. One Talmudic legend tells of a Roman emperor who was a frequent Sabbath guest in the house of a leading rabbi. He was so captivated by the gefilte fish that he asked his cook to prepare it for him, but although his cook kept exactly to the recipe supplied by the rabbi's cook, it turned out to lack the unique aroma and taste of the Sabbath dish at the rabbi's home. The disappointed emperor asked the rabbi for an explanation.

– Jews have a special spice, said the rabbi, and it alone gives the dish the flavour you like so much.

The emperor was taken aback and immediately asked what the spice was and where he could obtain it.

– It is very old, answered the rabbi, and it is called the Sabbath.

Rachal
(Baked Fish)

Peel the potatoes and cut them into very thin slices. Cut the onions into very thin rings and fry in the butter until golden. In a baking pan greased with butter place alternate layers of potato, fish and onions (starting and finishing with potato). Season each layer with salt and pepper to taste. Pour over the cream beaten with the eggs and a little salt. Bake in a medium oven for approx. 45 minutes, until the potatoes are a golden brown.

8–10 medium-sized potatoes

1–2 tablespoons butter

3 medium-sized onions

1/2 kg boiled fish (carp, cod or hake)

salt and ground pepper

1 1/2 cup cream

2 eggs

Mackerel with Garlic

Gut and wash the fish, and sprinkle inside and out with salt and pepper. Fry in very hot oil on both sides. Then reduce the heat a little. Add the thinly sliced garlic and the parsley root cut into julienne strips, and gently sauté them until golden brown. Sprinkle the fish with lemon juice and serve with potatoes and fresh or sterilised vegetables or salad.

1 kg small mackerel

salt and ground pepper

oil for frying

4–5 cloves of garlic

1 parsley root

juice of 1 lemon

There are many customs linked to Rosh Hashanah, the Jewish New Year. Apart from dipping the Challah and also pieces of apple in honey, so that the coming year will be sweet, fish-heads and carrots are served as symbols of fertility and hope. A ceremony for the casting away of sins, known as Tashlich, is held beside water in which fish live. After reciting the ritual verses people throw all the crumbs from their pockets. It is a symbolic expression of hope that they will succeed in casting away all their sins.

Photo on following pages: Gefilte fisch

Holishkes
(Stuffed Cabbage Leaves)

1 large white cabbage

salt

Stuffing:

3/4 kg minced beef

2 eggs

3 tablespoons water

2 cloves garlic

1 onion

4 tablespoons rice

about 1 teaspoon salt

about 1/2 teaspoon ground pepper

Sauce:

3/4 kg tomatoes

500 ml tomato juice

1 onion

1 garlic clove

about 1 tablespoon brown sugar

salt and ground pepper

Cut the stalk out of the cabbage. Blanche the cabbage in slightly salted boiling water, drain it and separate it into its individual leaves (an alternative is not to blanch it but pull off the leaves, leave them in the freezer for 2 days and then thaw them – they will be soft even without cooking). Thoroughly mix together the minced meat, eggs, cold water, crushed garlic, finely chopped onion, and rice, adding salt and pepper to taste. Put a spoonful of stuffing on each leaf and roll up. Then make the sauce by placing the peeled and chopped tomatoes, tomato juice, chopped onion, and crushed garlic in a pan, adding salt and pepper, and gently simmering for 15 minutes. Arrange the cabbage rolls in a baking dish, pour the tomato sauce over them and bake covered in a medium-hot oven for about an hour.

Variation: Omit the garlic from both sauce and filling. 30 minutes after putting the baking dish in the oven add about 3 tablespoons of honey, three tablespoons of lemon juice and 1/4 cup rinsed raisins. Then bake for another 30 minutes.

Holishkes is the traditional dish for the feast of Sukkot, also known as the harvest festival or Feast of Tabernacles. At this thanksgiving for the autumn harvest of the fields, gardens and vineyards, people move into tents erected in gardens or on balconies for seven days, in memory of the experiences of their forebears during their forty years in the desert. Traditionally it was not cabbage leaves but young vine leaves that were stuffed. We find similar recipes in Russia, where they are called galuptzi (pigeons) or in Greece, where they are known as dolmades.

Photo: Holishkes

UBERGINE BAKED WITH CHEESE

Cut the aubergine into rounds 1/2 cm thick and fry on both sides in oil. Arrange half the slices on the bottom of an oiled baking dish, sprinkle with salt and cover with a mixture of the beaten eggs, cheese, a pinch of salt and the rice. Arrange the rest of the slices on top, sprinkle with a little salt and with the chopped fresh herbs (dried herbs may be used instead), and cover this layer with slices of tomato. Add just a little more salt, dot with olive oil, and bake in a medium-hot oven for 45–50 minutes.

1 large aubergine
oil for frying
salt
4 eggs
1 cup grated cheese
1 cup cooked rice
1 sprig each of parsley, rosemary and basil
2 large tomatoes
1 tablespoon olive oil

AUBERGINE ROLLS WITH MEAT

Peel the aubergines and cut them into rounds 1 cm thick. Dip them in egg beaten with a little salt and fry them on both sides until golden. Then make the stuffing. Sauté the finely chopped onion and parsley in the oil used to fry the aubergines, add the minced meat and fry until brown (smooth out lumps with a fork). Let the mixture cool slightly and then add the remaining egg, rice, and salt and pepper to taste. Mix well. Place 1–2 teaspoons of stuffing on one edge of aubergine slice and roll up. Continue until all the materials are used up. Arrange the rolls in an oiled baking dish. Sprinkle them with a little sugar, and pour on water mixed with tomato juice. Dot with warmed poultry fat and bake in a preheated oven for 30–40 minutes.

2–3 aubergines
2–3 eggs
salt
2–3 tablespoons oil for frying
about 1/2 teaspoon sugar
1/4 cup water
1 cup tomato juice
1 tablespoon poultry fat
Stuffing:
1 onion
2 tablespoons finely chopped parsley root
1/2 kg minced beef
3 tablespoons rice
salt and ground pepper

The sukkah, or tent that is erected for the feast of Sukkot, is usually richly decorated with flowers and fruits. Peppers, aubergines, sweetcorn and white and blue grapes are hung on the walls, and in warm countries oranges, dates, figs and pomegranates. The dishes prepared on the festival days use all the available kinds of autumn vegetable and fruit as main ingredients. Tasty dishes made of glossy, purple aubergines are a prime example.

Photo: Aubergine Baked with Cheese

Farfel Stewed With Meat

1 cup coarse flour
1 cup semolina
2 eggs
1 tablespoon water
2 tablespoons poultry fat or oil
1/2 kg cooked poultry or beef
about 2 teaspoons salt
about 1/2 teaspoon ground pepper
2–3 cups stock

Work the sifted flour, semolina, egg and water into a very stiff dough. Divide it into 3 parts and knead each individually. If the dough is not firm enough, add a little more flour. Then grate the dough coarsely and leave it to dry out on the board overnight. The next day bake the farfel (dough) to a light brown in a low oven. Use a rolling pin to break up any large lumps. Then brown the farfel in the fat or oil in an oven-proof pan, add the cubed meat, season with salt and pepper to taste, add the stock and cook covered in a moderate oven until the farfel is soft and has absorbed all the liquid (take care not to allow the farfel to dry out too much, and if necessary add a little more water or stock). **Variation:** Farfel can also be prepared with smoked poultry, served as a side dish for meat or as an addition to soup (grate it more finely, and just let it dry out; then boil in salted water for about 10 minutes).

Stuffed Poultry Necks

4–5 poultry necks (turkey, duck or goose)
1 bread roll
3–4 cloves of garlic
salt and ground pepper
1–2 tablespoons poultry fat

Carefully remove the skin from the necks and chop the meat with a sharp knife. Soak the bread roll in cold water and squeeze out. Mince up with the meat and then season the mixture with garlic crushed with salt, adding a little more salt and pepper to taste. Fill the skins of the necks with the meat mixture and sew up both ends with white thread. Rub salt and pepper on the outside of the filled necks, and bake them in the poultry fat in a preheated oven, basting when necessary.

Farfel – fluffed up, light fragments of noodle dough – is a dish mainly associated with the feast of Rosh Hashanah, when everyone is supposed to examine his soul and pray for the forgiveness of his sins. The farfel symbolises grains of corn as a promise of an abundant harvest in the next year.

Photo: Farfel Stewed with Meat

Kreplach
(Filled Pirozhki)

First make the filling. Finely chop the onion and fry in the oil until golden. Add the minced meat and fry for another 5 minutes (breaking up lumps with a fork). Add salt and pepper to the mixture to taste and allow to cool. Work the sifted flour, egg, water and salt into a firm but pliable dough and roll it out thinly. Then cut it into squares with sides 5–7 cm long and put a teaspoon of filling in the middle of each square. Fold over the dough to produce triangle shapes, and press the edges firmly together. Boil the pirozhki in salted water for 15–20 minutes, and then lift them out carefully with a perforated ladle and allow to drain. Serve the kreplach as a separate dish sprinkled with fried bread-crumbs and dotted with warm poultry fat, or as an addition to soup (goldene jojch – see recipe on p. 8).

Variation: Instead of boiling kreplach, we can fry it in oil on both sides until golden. Tasty additions to the meat filling include crushed garlic or finely chopped parsley or chives. An alternative to the traditional meat filling is cottage cheese (quark) filling (mix soft quark with finely chopped onion fried in poultry fat, 1 egg, a little mashed potato and salt to taste).

Dough:

1 cup semi-coarse flour

1 egg

1–2 tablespoons water

1/4 teaspoon salt

Filling:

1 onion

1 tablespoon oil

1 cup minced cooked beef, chicken or turkey meat

salt and ground pepper

Kreplach is served on the eve of the feast of Yom Kippur, the most solemn event in the Jewish calendar. This Day of Atonement or Sabbath of Sabbaths is a day of rest from every kind of work, a day of strict fasting and repentance before God, when Jews must search their consciences, acknowledge their sins and pray for forgiveness. The meat filling of the kreplach symbolises the strict justice of the Lord, who on Yom Kippur will make a final judgment on each person, and the thin, fine dough represents the kindness and mercy that overlays the strictness of his judgement.

Photo: Boiled Kreplach with Breadcrumbs (below) and Fried Kreplach

Matzos Baked with Spinach and Meat

1 onion
5–6 tablespoons oil
300 g minced beef
salt and ground pepper
1/2 kg frozen or fresh spinach
about 1 cup cooked and mashed potatoes
3 eggs
3 cloves of garlic
3–4 matzos

Soften the chopped onion in about 2 tablespoons of oil. Add the meat, salt and pepper to taste, and brown (break up lumps with a fork). Drain off any liquid and mix with the slightly thawed spinach (fresh spinach must be steamed and chopped), potato, 2 beaten eggs and the crushed garlic. Soak the matzos in cold water and when soft, dry them on a paper napkin (be careful, since they tear easily!). Place 2 matzos on the bottom of a baking dish greased with half the remaining oil, and spread the meat and spinach over them. Top with 1–2 matzos, spoon over the remaining egg beaten with a little salt and dot with the remaining oil. Bake until golden in a preheated oven.

Kasha varnishkes (Buckwheat and Mushrooms)

1 cup buckwheat
1 egg
3–4 tablespoons oil
1 onion
2 tablespoons finely chopped parsley root
1/2 kg fresh or about 2 cups soaked dried mushrooms
2 cups stock
salt and ground pepper
a pinch of chilli powder (optional)

Mix the buckwheat with the beaten egg and leave to stand for about an hour. Heat the oil, fry the chopped onion. Add first the parsley and then the chopped mushrooms, and fry for about another 10 minutes. Add and sauté the buckwheat, stirring continuously. Then add the heated stock, with salt and pepper, and the chilli. Simmer the buckwheat and mushroom covered for 15–20 minutes until the liquid has evaporated and the buckwheat is soft (but it should not be allowed to dry out, and a little extra water can be added if necessary). Serve the kasha separately or mixed with boiled broad noodles in a ratio of 1:1.

Filled matzos (minas) are a favourite Passover dish of the Sephardic Jews, especially in Turkey and Greece. There are innumerable variations. Fillings can also be made from poultry meat, and from fresh or dried mushrooms, and matzos with quark or cheese are delicious.

Photo: Matzos Baked with Spinach and Meat

Potato Knishes with Liver

Boil the potatoes in their skins, then peel and allow to cool. Grate (approx. 2 cups) and place on a board. Add the eggs, oil, sifted flour, potato flour, grated onion and salt and pepper to taste, and work into a firm dough. Then brown the chicken livers in oil, season with salt and pepper, allow to cool, and mince. Roll the dough out until about 3 cm thick and cut out squares with sides of about 4 cm. In the middle of each square make a hollow, press 1–2 teaspoons of filling into each hollow and decorate as you wish. Place the squares on a greased baking tray, brush with the egg yolk (beaten with a little water if you wish), and bake for 20 minutes in a medium oven.

Dough:
6–8 potatoes
2 eggs
2 tablespoons oil
1/2 cup coarse flour
1 tablespoon potato flour
1 onion
salt and ground pepper
1 egg yolk

Filling:
1 tablespoon oil
300 g chicken livers
salt and ground pepper

Knishes with Meat Filling

Add baking powder and salt to the sifted flour. Pour in the eggs beaten with oil and water and work into an elastic dough. Roll it out thin, brush with oil, and cut into rounds 6 cm in diameter. Mix the meat with onion fried in oil and add salt and ground pepper. Place a teaspoonful of filling in the centre of each round. Tweak the edges up and together to make triangles in which the filling is still visible. Decorate the knishes and bake on a greased tray for 35 minutes.

Dough
2 1/2 cups flour
1 teaspoon baking powder
1/2 teaspoon salt
2 eggs
2/3 cup oil
2 tablespoons water
oil for brushing

Filling:
1 1/2 cup minced cooked poultry or beef
2 onions
1–2 tablespoons oil
salt and ground pepper

Mr. Feldman calls the waiter and orders fish soup.

– I'm sorry, but they didn't deliver the fish – the waiter apologises.

– So you don't even have gefilte fish. Bring me some latkes then.

– The potatoes were black, rotten, we threw them out…

– So not even potato kugel then. All right. I'll have the chicken stewed with plums, and farfel…

– We're out of plums. But we do have knishes with meat filling.

– Oh very well then.

As the waiter goes off he says to himself – I'd like to have seen him eat all of that, if we'd had it!

Photo: Potato Knishes with Liver (above) and Knishes with Meat Filling

Potato Roll

Dough:
3/4 kg potatoes
1 1/2–2 cups coarse flour
1/2 cup semolina
2 tablespoons potato flour
1 egg
about 1 teaspoon salt
Filling:
400 g smoked poultry meat

Boil the potatoes in their skins. Allow to cool and then grate. Put all the dough ingredients together and work into a firm dough on a board. Roll it out into a square about 1 1/2 cm thick and sprinkle a layer of smoked poultry meat on half of it. Roll up the square tightly and seal firmly at each end. Wrap the roll in a wet teacloth, carefully transfer to a roasting pan and add enough boiling water to come halfway up the roll. Cover the pan and simmer gently for about 25 minutes. Then turn the roll over and simmer for another 20 minutes. Return the roll to the board and let the steam evaporate. Then remove the teacloth and slice the roll into rounds. Serve with stewed sauerkraut. The roll is excellent the next day as well, fried in oil.

Potato Triangles

1 kg potatoes
2–3 eggs
6 tablespoons coarse flour
2 tablespoons potato flour
about 1 teaspoon salt
2 eggs
breadcrumbs
oil for frying
Filling:
1 tablespoon oil
1 onion
1/2 kg minced beef
5 cloves of garlic
1 sweet pepper
salt and ground pepper

Photo: Potato Roll

Fry the chopped onion in oil. Add and brown the meat (breaking up lumps with a fork). Add the crushed garlic, the chopped sweet pepper, salt and pepper to taste, and fry until soft. Boil the potatoes in their skins, peel and allow to cool. Grate the potatoes and mix with the egg, flour, potato flour and salt, working the mixture into a dough. Roll out the dough to approx. 1/2 cm thick and cut out squares with sides of approx. 10 cm. Place a teaspoon of filling on each square, fold them into triangle shapes and firmly press down the edges. Dip the triangles in egg beaten with a little water, coat in breadcrumbs, and fry in hot oil until golden.

Although it is primarily latkes – potato but also cheese pancakes fried in oil – that are traditionally served on the feast of Chanukah, potato triangles or a potato roll, all fried in oil, are also reminders of the miraculous jug of oil for lighting the candlestick in the Temple.

Latkes (Potato Pancakes)

Peel potatoes raw and grate finely (some of the water can be squeezed out into a bowl and allowed to stand; it can then be drained off leaving the starch which can be returned to the potatoes). Add the finely chopped onion, eggs, matzo or semi-coarse flour, and salt and pepper. Mix well. Heat the oil and fry the mixture in spoonfuls, using the back of the spoon to flatten the pancakes. Fry on both sides until golden.

Variation: A little grated cheese may be added to the latke mixture, or crushed garlic used instead of onion. In Jewish cuisine potato pancakes are also served with jam or melted chocolate (use less salt and pepper).

5 large potatoes

1 onion

4 eggs

1/4 cup matzo or semi-coarse flour

salt and ground pepper

oil for frying

Cheese Latkes

Mix together all the ingredients except the oil and jam. Put spoonfuls of the mixture into the hot oil and fry on both sides until golden. While the cheese latkes are still hot, spread them with cherry or other sharp jam and serve immediately.

3 eggs

1/4 cup water

1 1/2 cup grated cheese

1/2 cup semi-coarse flour

3 tablespoons milk

2 tablespoons sugar

pinch of salt and ground pepper

oil for frying

cherry jam to serve

The Jews probably took over potato pancakes in the 17th century in the Ukraine, where they were a popular side dish for the Christmas goose. The cheese pancakes recall the heroic deed of the legendary Judith, who was endowed not just with beauty but with intelligence. When Nebuchadnezzar's general Holofernes lusted after her, Judith fed him salt cheese, which made him very thirsty. He drowned his thirst in many goblets of wine, fell deeply asleep, and Judith cut off his head. She took it to show his soldiers in Jerusalem, and they fled in horror at his fate.

Photo: Cheese Latkes

POTATO KUGEL

6–7 medium large
potatoes
1 onion
1/2 cup matzo meal
6–7 tablespoons oil
2 eggs
about 2 teaspoons
salt

Peel and grate the potatoes raw. Add the finely chopped or grated onion, matzo meal, oil, eggs and salt, and mix well. Heat the form or baking dish at low temperature in a preheated oven. Then pour the dough into the hot form or baking dish and bake for 45 minutes until the kugel is golden and crispy. Serve separately or as an accompaniment to meat.

ONION KUGEL

6 eggs
3 cups finely
chopped onion
5 tablespoons
breadcrumbs
1 1/2 teaspoons salt
1/2 teaspoon ground
pepper
4 tablespoons melted
butter or poultry fat

Beat the egg yolks to a thick pale foam, add the chopped onion, sifted flour, salt and pepper. Fold in the melted butter or fat and finally the white of egg whipped until stiff. Spread the dough in a greased form and bake in an oven preheated to 180 °C for about 45 minutes, until golden brown on top.

Kugel is a famous traditional festival food. The name is not derived from the German "die Kugel" (ball) as it might at first appear, but from the Hebrew "agol" meaning "round". Originally kugels were indeed round, but in the course of time Jewish housewives forgot the reason for the name and today we find kugels in all possible shapes. The kugel has many variants not only of form but also of flavour. There are kugels based on potato, rice or noodles, sweet or savoury kugels, meat or vegetable, and kugels flavoured with pineapple or nuts, honey, raisins or apples.

Rice Kugel

Boil the rice for about 10 minutes in slightly salted water. Then drain, allow to dry off and cool. Whip the eggs with the sugar to a foam. Add the rice, the sliced and peeled apples, the rinsed raisins, cinnamon and melted butter, and lightly mix together. Put the mixture in a greased dish and bake for approx. 40 minutes until golden in an oven pre-heated to 180°C. Serve the kugel decorated with fresh or tinned fruit or a fruit salad.

1 1/2 cup rice

salt

6 eggs

6 tablespoons icing sugar

3 apples

1 cup raisins

2 teaspoons ground cinnamon

5 tablespoons melted butter

Cabbage Kugel

Sprinkle salt on the cabbage simmer gently in the butter for 30 minutes. Pour hot water on the diced bread and then squeeze it out and mix with the potato flour, sugar and whipped yolks of egg. Add the rinsed raisins and finely chopped peeled almonds. Combine the mixture with the stewed and cooled cabbage. Finally fold in the eggwhites, whipped until stiff, and put the mixture in a greased form. Bake the cabbage kugel in an oven preheated to 180°C for about 40 minutes until golden.

5 cups finely chopped white cabbage

about 2 teaspoons salt

5 tablespoons melted butter

1 1/2 cup cubed bread

1/2 cup water

5 tablespoons potato flour

2 tablespoons icing sugar

4 eggs

4–5 tablespoons raisins

3/4 cup almonds

– You don't believe in God?
– No, but I do believe in resurrection.
– That's completely illogical, isn't it?
– Well look here, when on the Sabbath a Jew pours so much wine, spirits and tea down his throat, and stuffs himself with goldene jojch and kreplach, gefilte fish, schollet and goose, tzimmes, blintzes, kugel... falls dead on the sofa, has forty winks and then gets up quite as normal, there can be no doubt about resurrection.

Photo on following pages: Rice, Cabbage and Potato Kugel (from left to right)

33

SCHOLLET WITH GOOSE

1 goose (weighing about 2 kg)

about 2 teaspoons salt

2 tablespoons goose fat or oil

1 large onion

2 cups dried beans

2 cups barley

5 cloves of garlic

1/2 teaspoon ginger

1/2 teaspoon ground pepper

stock for stewing

Cut the goose into portions, rub with salt inside and out and brown on all sides in melted goose fat or oil. Remove the goose and fry the onions in the same fat. Put the goose with the onions in a roasting pan or casserole, and surround with a mixture of the beans and barley (previously soaked). Add crushed garlic and ginger, add pepper, pour in the stock (water may be used instead) and cook gently either on top of the stove or inside the oven for about 2 hours until soft. During the cooking add more stock as necessary. In the end add salt to the schollet to taste. If making schollet on Friday according to Jewish custom, keep warm until the next day in a very low oven.

Variation: Dried peas can be substituted for beans in the schollet, and sweet or hot ground paprika can be used to flavour it. The ratio of pulses to barley can be changed to 3:1, i.e. 3 cups beans or peas to 1 cup barley.

Schollet has been known since the earliest times. We meet it in the Talmud under the name of chamin – warm. Later in Europe the names scholet or schallet (from the French chaud – hot) were used for the dish, and in East Europe chulent or schulent. It is possible that the name schollet comes from the Yiddish word "schul-end", meaning the end of the Sabbath morning service, and so the time to sit down to the festive schollet. As soon as the family had returned from the synagogue and sat down, the wife would bring the large pot of sweet-smelling schollet from the oven, where it had been keeping warm since Friday. The making of a fire on the Sabbath was forbidden, and so the schollet had to be prepared a day early. Housewives also saved themselves work by sending the pots of schollet to the bakery, where the food would stew gently overnight in a large oven. After the morning service errand boys would deliver the cooked schollet or the children would be sent to get it. This joint preparation of schollet was a custom in the Prague Ghetto as well. In the countryside housewives would often save themselves work by putting the schollet pot under feather guilts to keep warm until the next day.

Photo: Schollet with Goose

Schollet with Dumplings

Cube the meat and brown in the oil. Add the chopped onion, add salt and pepper and set aside. Peel the potatoes (halve them if large), and put them with the butter in a roasting dish or thick-sided casserole. Add the pre-soaked haricot beans and barley together with the crushed garlic, and pour on the stock (or water) until it just covers the ingredients. Cook gently for 2–3 hours, adding more water when necessary. Meanwhile make whichever dumpling you choose. For matzo dumplings first whip the eggs, add the oil, cold water, salt and gradually the matzo meal. Work into a dough, place in the fridge to chill for 20 minutes, then take out and make into a dumpling roll. For meat dumplings soak the bread in cold water, squeeze out and add the meat, egg, nutmeg, crushed garlic, salt, pepper and parsley. Make a dumpling roll. Put the matzo or meat dumpling into the schollet and cook at a very low heat (approx. 120°C) overnight.

– Listen Rosa – said poor Rosenzweig to his wife – rich Jews spend their whole lives stuffing themselves with schollet. What if we were to make ourselves schollet just once, at least for our Diamond Wedding anniversary?

– We could – replied Rosa – but we don't have beans or peas.

– So use lentils.

Rosa goes to the kitchen but soon comes back:

– But we don't have any beef either.

– So use sausages.

Rosa nods, goes off, but is back again after a few minutes.

– There's not a trace of goose fat in the house.

– But you've got suet, haven't you?

– I've discovered we haven't got the spices, either.

– Stop fussing. Just leave out the spices.

– There's no onion or garlic.

– Thrown in a bit of cut grass.

Finally they sit down at table and Rosenzweig tries the schollet:

– I don't know what these rich Jews see in this schollet.

1/2 kg beef

2 tablespoons oil

1 onion

about 2 teaspoons salt

1/2 teaspoon ground pepper

6 small potatoes

4 cloves of garlic

1 cup haricot beans

1/2 cup barley

stock

Matzo Dumplings:

2 eggs

2 tablespoons oil

2 tablespoons water

1/2 teaspoons salt

3/4 cup matzo meal

Meat Dumplings:

1 cup breadcrumbs

1 cup minced beef

1 egg

1/4–1/2 teaspoon grated nutmeg

3 cloves of garlic

about 1/2 teaspoon salt

about 1/4 teaspoon ground pepper

1 tablespoon finely chopped parsley

Photo: Schollet with Matzo Dumplings

CHICKEN STEWED WITH PRUNES

2 tablespoons oil

1 onion

1 chicken (weighing about 1 1/2 kg)

1 cup water

3 teaspoons ground cinnamon

1 teaspoon ginger

1/2 teaspoon ground pepper

about 1 teaspoons salt

2 cups prunes

about 1 tablespoon brown sugar or honey

1/2 cup almonds

Lightly fry the chopped onion in the oil, then push it to one side and add the chicken cut into portions. Brown them on all sides. Add the water mixed with cinnamon, the ginger, pepper and salt and bring to the boil. Then reduce the temperature and simmer covered for approx. 30 minutes. Arrange the stoned, soaked prunes around the chicken (they should be submerged in the liquid, and so add water if necessary). Flavour with the sugar or honey and simmer for another about 20 minutes until the chicken is tender. In the meantime scald and peel the almonds, roast them in a low oven, and add them to the stew when it is nearly ready. Arrange the chicken and prunes on a plate and pour over the sauce. Serve with steamed rice or farfel (see recipe on p. 20).

BAKED CHICKEN IN HONEY

1 chicken (weighing about 1 1/2–2 kg)

about 1 teaspoon salt

1/2 teaspoon ground pepper

lemon juice

4–5 tablespoons warm vegetable oil

4 tablespoons honey

1/4–1/2 teaspoon grated nutmeg

Rub the chicken with salt and pepper and sprinkle with lemon juice. Mix the melted vegetable fat with the honey and nutmeg in a bowl and coat the chicken with the mixture inside and out. Put the chicken in a roasting dish, pour the remaining fat and honey over it, add water to prevent drying out, and roast in a preheated oven for about an hour until golden. Baste the chicken frequently in its juices while cooking, and add water if necessary. Serve with boiled potatoes and finely chopped parsley.

Although Jewish Kosher cuisine uses neither bacon nor ordinary or soured cream in the preparation of meat, the food is rich, varied in taste and full of surprising ideas. While the Jewish housewife cooks using recipes traditional in her family, she also reworks them before handing them on to her children. This is what makes Jewish cuisine so full of variation and modification, so that there are all kinds of family, local, regional and historical versions of a single dish.

Photo: Chicken Stewed with Prunes

Duck with Apple Stuffing

Rub the duck inside and out with a paste made of garlic crushed with salt and pepper, and then prick the skin lightly with a fork. Coarsely chop the prunes (having previously soaked them in water) and add the peeled diced apple, egg, sieved breadcrumbs and sugar. Mix well. Stuff the duck and sew up with white thread.

Put the duck in a preheated oven and roast it for about 30 minutes at 200°C, then reduce the temperature and roast until tender, basting frequently and adding water if necessary. If the duck is fatty, gradually spoon off the fat. Serve with boiled potatoes and finely chopped parsley.

1 duck (weighing about 1 1/2–2 kg)

2–3 cloves of garlic

2 teaspoons salt

1/4 teaspoon ground pepper

Stuffing:

12 prunes

2–3 apples

1 egg

4 tablespoons breadcrumbs

1–2 tablespoons sugar

Stuffed Turkey Breast

Fry the onion lightly in fat or oil. Add the farfel, fry quickly and add the stock (water may be used instead). Add salt, pepper and nutmeg and simmer gently. In the meantime boil the carrot and celeriac until half-cooked and then coarsely grate them into the farfel. Add the chopped parsley, mix and allow to cool a little.

Cut the turkey breasts into a single flat slice and tenderise. Sprinkle slightly with salt and spread with the stuffing. Roll up the meat and secure with white thread. Roast the stuffed turkey roll for 40–50 minutes until tender. During roasting baste in its own juices and add more stock or water when necessary.

about 1/2 kg turkey breasts

salt

Stuffing:

1–2 tablespoons fat or oil

1 onion

1 cup farfel (see recipe on p. 20)

1 cup stock

salt and ground pepper

pinch of grated nutmeg

1 carrot

1/4 celeriac

1/2 cup finely chopped parsley

Many Jewish dishes are flavoured with garlic, which is an integral element of kosher cuisine. According to the Talmud, which strongly recommends garlic, the bulb with its strong taste and intense smell has five properties: it is filling, it warms the body, lights up the face, multiplies the seed and eliminates worms in the bowels.

Photo: Duck with Apple Stuffing

43

Meat and Prune Tzimmes

1–1 1/2 kg beef
about 250 g prunes
1–2 onions
salt and ground pepper
2 tablespoons oil
1 1/2 tablespoons coarse flour
juice of 1 lemon
about 1 tablespoon sugar
6–8 potatoes

Pour enough water over the meat to cover it, add the soaked and stoned prunes and whole onions, season with salt and pepper to taste and cook until the meat is tender. Heat the oil in a pan, add flour to make a light roux and then gradually pour in 2–3 cups of the strained meat stock, stirring continuously. Simmer briefly, add the lemon juice and sugar and cook for about another 3 minutes. Then place slices of peeled potato on the bottom of a large casserole and arrange portions of the meat and the prunes on top. Pour the strained sauce over the meat and cook covered for about 40 minutes in a medium hot oven. Add more stock during the cooking if necessary.

Picadillo
(Spicy Meat with Olives)

1–2 tablespoons oil
1 onion
3 cloves of garlic
1 kg minced beef
1/2 kg tomatoes
2 apples
1 green pepper
1/2 cup raisins
1/2 teaspoon ground chilli powder
1/2 teaspoon ground cinnamon
salt and ground pepper
2/3 cup green olives

Fry the chopped onions and crushed garlic. Add the meat and brown (breaking up lumps with a fork). Gradually add the chopped peeled tomato, cubed apple and pepper, rinsed raisins, chilli and cinnamon with salt and pepper to taste, and gently stew, covered, for about 30 minutes. When the liquid has evaporated, add the olives and cook just a little longer. Serve with rice.

Cinnamon, a spice with a distinctive aroma and sweet taste, is actually the bark of a small ever-green tropical tree or bush, twisted into rolls. One of the oldest known spices, it is mentioned in the Bible and used mainly to flavour cakes, pastries and puddings. In Jewish cuisine, however, and other cuisines of the Middle East, it is also often used to flavour stewed meat or poultry stuffings.

Photo: Picadillo

CARROT TZIMMES

Cut the carrots into rounds and fry briefly in melted butter (or vegetable fat). Then just cover with water, add salt, sugar, honey and cinnamon and stew gently, covered, until soft. Finally flavour the carrot tzimmes with fresh orange juice and more sugar if desired.

Variations: Peeled and sliced apples may be substituted for a third of the carrots. Add them when the carrots are half-cooked, so that they don't disintegrate with cooking.

1 kg carrots

1–2 tablespoons butter

about 1 teaspoon salt

about 1 teaspoon sugar

1 tablespoon honey

1/2 teaspoon ground cinnamon

1–2 tablespoons orange juice

PRUNE TZIMMES

Rinse the prunes, cover with hot water and leave for about an hour to swell. Then pour off the water, stone the prunes, put them in an oven-proof pan with 4 cups of boiling water and bring back to the boil. Add the farfel, salt, lemon juice, honey and butter (or vegetable fat). Cover the pan and place in an oven preheated to 180°C. After half an hour remove the lid and bake the tzimmes for about another 15 minutes.

1/2 kg dried prunes

4 cups water

1 cup farfel (see recipe on p. 20)

about 1 teaspoon salt

2 tablespoons lemon juice

1/3 cup honey

4 tablespoons melted butter

Tzimmes are among the sweetest of Jewish dishes. They are so popular that the expression "tzimmes" had acquired broader meanings in conversational Yiddish. To "do tzimmes with someone" means to pay him too much attention and make a great fuss of him (it used to require a lot of time and attention to cook tzimmes). The name tzimmes is usually considered to derive from the word tzimmt – cinnamon. The dish is well-known for its multiplicity of variants. The most common are carrot tzimmes or tzimmes made of dried fruit, but they can also be made from potatoes, or even with meat (see recipe on p. 44), but they all contain quite a lot of sugar or honey. Tzimmes are a popular dish on every feast, and at Rosh Hashanah have the symbolic meaning of bringing more hope to the New Year with their sweetness.

Photo: Carrot Tzimmes (below) and Prune Tzimmes

Varenikes
(Pirozhki with Cherries)

dough as
for kreplach (see
recipe on p. 23)

salt

1 cup sour cream for
serving

Filling:

about 3 cups tinned
cherries

juice from 1 tin
of cherries

1/2–3/4 cup sugar

2 teaspoons lemon
juice

about 1 teaspoon
potato flour

about 1 tablespoon
water

Put the stoned cherries and juice from the tin in a pan. According to taste add sugar and lemon juice (optional), bring to the boil and simmer on a low heat for 5–8 minutes. Then add the potato flour mixed in water and cook briefly (not more than 2 minutes, or the potato flour will lose its capacity to thicken). Drain the cherries and allow to cool, reserving the juice. Roll out the kreplach dough thinly and cut rounds out of it. Put a teaspoon of cherry on each round, close up the dough round the filling and press the edges firmly together. Boil the pirozhki in lightly salted water until they float to the surface. To serve, pour over the thickened cherry juice and decorate with a dollop of sour cream.

Variation: Fruit pirozhkis can also be made from fresh cherries, using freshly squeezed out cherry juice instead of canned juice. The flavour and aroma will be enhanced. Another variation is to use tinned apricots. Or add pomegranate juice to the sauce.

Figs, grapes, dates and above all pomegranates were favourite fruits in old Jewish cuisine. Pomegranates, which contain a large number of seeds enclosed in juicy red flesh, have a bitter-sweet taste and are a symbol of fertility. They were used to make a thick syrup to be poured over dishes or used as a dip for bread.

*Photo: Varenikes
with Cherries*

Milchidike lokschen kugel (Noodle Kugel)

Beat the egg yolks and sugar into a thick pale foam. Then gradually mix in the soft cottage cheese, milk, 5 tablespoons of warm butter (vegetable fat may also be used), rinsed raisins and chopped pitted prunes. At the end lightly fold in the coarsely grated apple, cooked drained noodles, and egg whites beaten until stiff. Place the dough in a greased form, sprinkle with cinnamon mixed with sugar and dot with the remaining butter (or vegetable fat). Bake for about 45 minutes until golden in a preheated oven at medium heat.

3 eggs

3 tablespoons sugar

2 cups cottage cheese

1 cup milk

6–7 tablespoons melted butter

1 cup raisins

15 dried prunes

5 apples

400 g cooked thin noodles

2 tablespoons cinnamon and 6 tablespoons sugar

Quick Cheese Blintzes

Mix together the flour, baking powder, vanilla sugar, cream, eggs and butter and work into a smooth batter gradually adding milk. Pour about 1 1/2 cups of batter into a greased baking form and bake for about 20 minutes in a pre-heated medium oven. Meanwhile make the filling. Mix the cheese, sugar and eggs until smooth. Carefully spoon the filling onto the baked batter, smooth the surface and pour the remaining batter over the filling. Bake for another about 40 minutes until golden. Serve decorated with fruit.
Variation: Blintzes are traditionally made in the form of individual pancakes and are filled only after baking.

1 1/3 cup semi-coarse flour

1 1/4 teaspoon baking powder

1 tablespoon vanilla sugar

2 tablespoons sour cream

4 large eggs

1/4 cup melted butter

1 1/4 cup milk

Filling:

2 1/2 cups cottage cheese

1 cup cream cheese

about 3 tablespoons sugar

2 eggs

On the feast of Shavuot dairy dishes like cheese blintzes, festival kugel with cheese and milk, kreplach with cream cheese filling or cheesecakes are served. They symbolically recall the events on Mount Sinai, where the Lord gave Moses the Torah, in which the land of Israel is described as a land overflowing with milk and honey. The cakes are often shaped like the tablets on which the Ten Commandments were inscribed, or made into cone shapes reminiscent of Mount Sinai.

Photo: Quick Cheese Blintzes

51

CHEESECAKE

5 eggs
1 cup sugar
2 tablespoons fine flour
2 1/2 cups cottage or curd cheese
3/4 cup sour cream
1 vanilla sugar
6 tablespoons raisins

Beat the egg yolks with the sugar into a thick pale foam. Add the flour, cheese, sour cream, vanilla sugar and rinsed raisins. Beat the egg-whites until stiff and fold in.

Pour the mixture into a greased and floured baking tin and bake for about 30 minutes in a preheated oven. Let the cake cool in the oven.

LEKACH (HONEYCAKE)

1 cup strong coffee
1 3/4 cup honey
3 tablespoons brandy
4 eggs
1 1/4 cup brown sugar
4 tablespoons oil
3 1/2 cups fine flour
3 teaspoons baking powder
1 teaspoon baking soda
1 teaspoon cinnamon
1/4 teaspoon ground cloves
1/4 teaspoon grated nutmeg
1/2 teaspoon ginger
1 cup walnuts
1 cup raisins
2 tablespoons candied lemon peel

Melt the honey with the coffee in a pan, mix well, bring to the boil and set aside. When cool add the brandy (optional). Beat the eggs in a large bowl with the sugar, gradually pouring in the oil while beating. Then alternately add the flour sieved with the baking powder, baking soda and the coffee, honey and brandy mixture. Finally add the spices, finely chopped walnuts and finely chopped candied lemon peel. Pour the mixture into a greased and floured baking tin and bake for about 70 minutes at a temperature of 200°C. Serve the next day.

Lekach, meaning honey-cake, is the traditional sweetmeat of East European Jews. It is served at the feast of Rosh Hashanah as a symbol of a good and sweet new year, but is also prepared for major family celebrations such as birthdays, barmitzvahs (the coming of age of thirteen-year-old boys as members of the Jewish community), engagements and weddings…

Photo: Lekach

Pesach Banana Cake

Beat the egg yolks with the sugar and pinch of salt into a thick pale foam. Add the mashed bananas, potato flour and coarsely chopped walnuts. Finally beat the whites of eggs until stiff and fold into the mixture. Butter a cake tin and line it with matzo meal, press the mixture into the tin and bake in a preheated oven for 50–60 minutes. Leave the cake in the tin. After 30 minutes cover it in aluminium foil and leave overnight in a cool place. On the next day cut the cake, spread with half of the stiffly whipped cream (adding a thickening agent if desired), top with rounds of banana and decorate with remaining cream.

7 eggs
1 cup castor sugar
pinch of salt
1 cup mashed bananas
3/4 cup potato flour
1 cup walnuts
cream and 2–3 bananas for decoration

Matzaloksh (Matzo Cake)

Beat the egg yolks with the sugar to a thick pale foam. Add the matzo meal, lemon and orange juice, ground nuts and coarsely grated apple. Place the mixture in a tin that has been buttered and sprinkled with matzo meal and bake in a preheated oven for about 45 minutes. Meanwhile make the chocolate icing. Blend the sugar with the vegetable fat. Melt the chocolate into the coffee in a bowl over hot waters, stirring continuously, and then gradually mix it into the sugar and fat. Finally add one yolk after another and mix until the icing is smooth. Then put it in the fridge. When the cake is cool, cut it and spread with a thick layer of jam. Spread the chocolate icing on the top of the cake.

6 eggs
6 tablespoons castor sugar
6 tablespoons matzo meal
1 lemon
1 orange
50 g walnuts
1 apple
redcurrant or blackcurrant jam
Chocolate Icing:
3/4 cup castor sugar
9 tablespoons vegetable fat
100 g chocolate
2 tablespoons strong coffee
2 egg yolks

Photo: Pesach Banana Cake

The cake known as Matzaloksh, made from matzo meal, is a traditional part of the celebratory seder dinner on the feast of Pesach. Another variant of the festive seder cake is banana cake with cream.

Hamentaschen
(Haman Pastries)

Pastry:

1/2 cup softened butter

1/4 cup brown sugar

1/4 cup honey

2 large eggs

1 vanilla sugar

2 1/2 cups fine flour

1 teaspoon baking powder

1/2 teaspoon baking soda

Poppy-seed Filling:

1/4 cup water

3/4 cup sugar

200 g poppy seed

1 egg white

1 vanilla sugar

juice of 1/2 lemon and 1/2 orange

1 tablespoon rum

1 cup raisins

1/4 teaspoon ground cinnamon

1 cup apricot jam

1/4 cup softened butter

Blend the butter (vegetable fat may be substituted) with the sugar and honey. Add the whipped eggs and vanilla sugar and gradually add the sieved flour mixed with the baking powder and baking soda. Work into a smooth dough and put in the fridge for 2–3 hours wrapped in aluminium foil. In the meantime prepare the poppy-seed filling. Heat the water with the sugar and ground poppy-seed on a low flame. After a while add the egg white, vanilla sugar, lemon and orange juice, rum, rinsed raisins and cinnamon and simmer for about 5 minutes while stirring continuously. Mix in the apricot jam (raspberry jam is also delicious), and the butter (or vegetable fat), and simmer until the fat has dissolved. Set aside and when it has cooled slightly put it in the fridge for a while. Roll the pastry into a sheet 1/2 cm thick and cut it into squares with sides of 10 cm. Put a heaped teaspoon of filling onto each square, fold up the pastry to create triangles and press the edges together firmly. Bake the triangles on a greased baking sheet in a preheated moderate oven for about 20 minutes until golden.

Variation: Cut circles out of the pastry, put a teaspoon of filling on each and press the edges of the pastry in to create triangles in which the filling is still visible in the middle.

Hamentaschen, the pastries associated with the feast of Purim, are traditionally cooked with poppy-seed filling. There are other variants, however, such as walnut filling (see recipe on p. 57) and damson cheese hamentaschen (mix 2 cups of damson cheese with the juice of half an orange and 1/2 cup of ground almonds or walnuts), supposedly baked in memory of a damson cheese seller from Mladá Boleslav, who was accused at the time of Purim of the premeditated murder of a customer. Fortunately the court found him innocent.

F LUDEN

Crumble the yeast into the warm, slightly sweetened milk and leave in a warm place to ferment. Then add the sieved flour, warmed butter (or vegetable fat), remaining sugar, beaten eggs and wine and work into a fine dough. Leave it to rise in a warm place for about an hour. Meanwhile make the fillings. For the walnut filling simply mix all ingredients. For the poppy-seed filling see p. 56. For the apple filling grate the apple coarsely and mix with the honey and cinnamon. When it is risen, divide the dough into 5 equal parts.

Roll out the first to the size of the baking sheet, transfer onto the greased baking sheet and spread with a thick layer of damson cheese. Roll out the next sheet, place on top and cover with a layer of walnut filling, and proceed in the same way with the next two sheets, spreading them with poppy-seed filling and apple filling respectively. Place the last sheet on the top and brush it with egg yolk beaten with a little sugar (1–2 teaspoons of water can be added), to create a glaze. Bake the cake for about 40 minutes until golden in a preheated oven.

Pastry:

1/4 cup milk

1/2 cup castor sugar

15–20 g yeast

4 cups semi-coarse flour

2 cups melted butter

4 eggs

8 tablespoons sweet wine

1 egg yolk and sugar for brushing

1 cup damson cheese

Walnut Filling:

1 cup ground walnuts

1 cup sugar

1 vanilla sugar

1/2 teaspoon ground cinnamon

juice of 1/2 lemon and 1/2 orange

1/4 cup raisins

1/2 cup apricot jam

Poppy-seed Filling:

see recipe on p. 56

Apple Filling:

4–5 apples

2 tablespoons honey

1 teaspoon ground cinnamon

Fluden is a rich, festive cake, usually baked for the feast of Simchat Torah (Rejoicing of the Torah) at the end of the festival of Sukkot. All the scrolls of the Torah are taken out of the Ark and the worshippers carry them seven times round the bimah, an elevated place in the middle of the synagogue. It is a happy occasion, with traditional Hebrew singing but also modern Hebrew and Yiddish songs and dances.

Photo on following pages: Hamentaschen (left) and Fluden

APPLE CAKE

6 apples
1 tablespoon sugar
1/2 teaspoon cinnamon
3 tablespoons orange juice
5 tablespoons flour
1 teaspoon baking powder
4 tablespoons butter
5 tablespoons brown sugar
1 egg
1/4 cup walnuts

Peel and core the apples and cut them in rounds. Sprinkle them with sugar and cinnamon and drops of orange juice. Lightly mix and place on bottom of a greased baking tin. Mix the sieved flour with the baking powder, add the butter (vegetable fat may be used instead) and rub into a breadcrumb texture with your fingertips. Then add the brown sugar, egg and chopped walnuts. Cover the apples with the mixture and bake in a preheated oven until the apples are soft and the top a golden brown.

CAKE WITH DRIED FRUIT AND ALMONDS

Bottom Half:
1/2 cup butter
1/4 cup sugar
1 cup semi-coarse flour

Top Half:
1/2 cup semi-coarse flour
1/2 teaspoon baking powder
2 tablespoons sugar
2 eggs
1 teaspoon vanilla sugar
1/2 cup dried apricots
1/2 cup dried figs
1/2 cup almonds

Beat the butter (vegetable fat may be substituted) with the sugar into a thick pale foam and then add the sieved flour. Press the mixture into a cake tin (there is no need to grease it) and bake for about 20 minutes in an oven preheated to 160°C. Meanwhile make the top half. Mix the sieved flour with the baking powder, sugar, eggs, vanilla sugar, finely chopped dried apricots and figs, and slivered almonds. Spread this mixture onto the half-baked mixture and bake until golden for about another 25 minutes. **Variation:** Other kinds of dried fruit such as prunes, dates, pears or apples can be used instead.

Little Isaac is praying to the Lord:
– Lord, I promise I will be obedient and good. But you must promise that you won't put vitamins in spinach, cabbage and carrots, but in chocolate, ice cream and cake.

Photo: Cake with Dried Fruit and Almonds

Apple Strudel

Mix the sifted flour with the pinch of salt and baking powder, egg beaten with warm water, vinegar and oil. Work into a smooth elastic dough (knead it for at least 10 minutes; the longer the dough is kneaded, the more it stretches) and leave it covered for 30 minutes in a warmed bowl (replace the warmed bowl as necessary). Then roll out the dough very thinly until almost transparent on a tea cloth dusted with flour. Cut off thicker edges and then spread or sprinkle with the breadcrumbs and chopped nuts. Arrange the apple slices on top, and sprinkle them with raisins and sugar mixed with cinnamon. Carefully lift up the cloth and roll the strudel down from it. Press in the edges to keep the filling from falling out. Using both hands carefully transfer the strudel to a greased baking sheet, brush it with oil or butter and bake in an oven preheated to about 180°C for roughly 45 minutes until golden. Dust with sugar and cut into slices while still hot.

2 1/2 cups fine flour

pinch of salt

1 teaspoon baking powder

1 egg

2/3 cup water

1 tablespoon vinegar

4 tablespoons oil

oil or melted butter for brushing

1 cup breadcrumbs

1 1/2 cup chopped walnuts

4 cups peeled cored apples cut into thin slices

1 cup raisins

1/2–3/4 cup sugar

2 teaspoons cinnamon

icing sugar for sprinkling

Apple Strudel is baked mainly on the feast of Sukkot, when it is traditionally served in all kinds of variants depending on the fruit and vegetables available. Strudel can be filled with stewed white cabbage, buckwheat and mushrooms (see recipe on p. 24) or cottage cheese – blend about 500 g cottage cheese with 1/2 cup sugar, 2 egg yolks, 1 vanilla sugar, the juice and peel of a well washed lemon, and finally the egg whites whipped until stiff.

Photo: Apple Strudel

INDEX